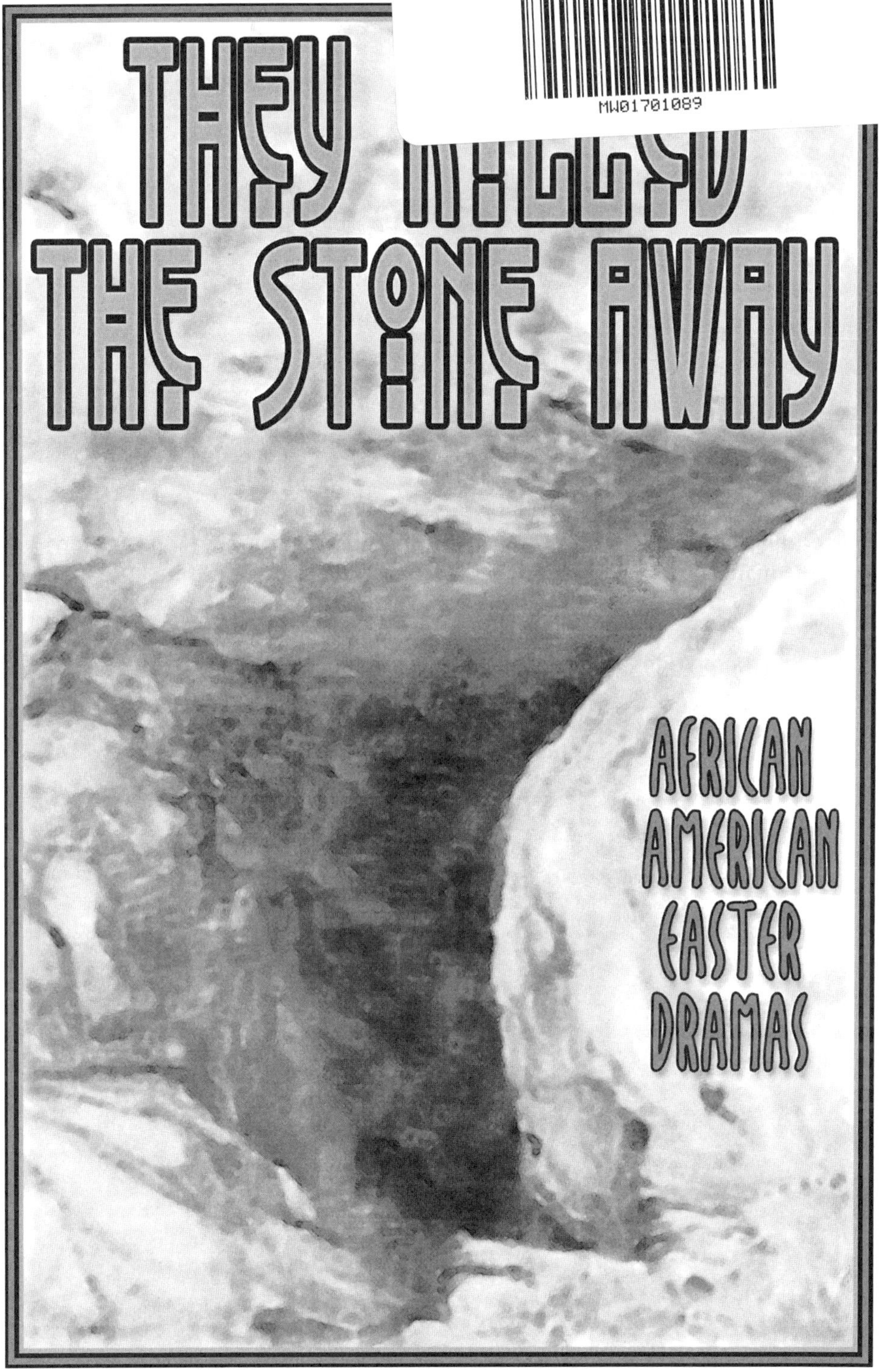

Abingdon Press
Nashville

THEY ROLLED THE STONE AWAY

ISBN 987-0-687-32839-0

08 09 10 11 12 13 14 15 16 17 - 10 9 8 7 6 5 4 3 2

Manufactured in the United States of America

CONTENTS

RESURRECTED LIVES

by Valeria Steele Roberson

CAST:

Mother: Alicia's mother
Alicia Carter: Young girl, age 9
Kim: Young girl, age 12
Bro. Joseph: Alicia's neighbor
Victoria: Young girl about age 9
Miss Julia: A lady in her 40's who hasn't been to church in many years
Off-stage female voice (OSF Voice): A woman's voice (any age)
Miss Owens: Director of Easter program
Soldier: One male—older child, teen, or adult
Joseph of Arimathea: Rich man, secret disciple of Jesus who buries him
Nicodemus: Follower of Jesus (No lines)
Mary, Mother of Jesus (Mary, Jesus): Middle-aged woman
Mary, Mother of Joses (Mary, Joses): Woman
Sister of Mary, Mother of Jesus (Sis of Mary): Woman
Mary Magdalene (Mary Mag.): Woman healed by Jesus
Salome: Follower of Jesus
Young Boy: Recitation done by a young boy with verbal skills
Stan Carter: Alicia's Daddy, a man
Kindergarten Class or any young students (KC/YS): Recitation done by kindergarten-aged children
Soldier: Young male
Angel: Young male

PROP LIST

Green plant
Bicycle
Bench
Purses for girls
Four chairs
Table
Newspaper
Jump rope
Soda pop
Money coins
Kim's watch
Spices for anointing Jesus' body
Loaf of bread
Old dress of Alicia's
Handkerchief of Jesus' mother

SET: The path to the church is shaped like a horseshoe. At upstage right, there is a bench that signifies Alicia's yard. Upstage-left, put a green plant, which stands for Miss Julia's yard. Place a bicycle downstage-left for Victoria's yard. As the girls arrive at the church, the stage is being prepared for the Easter Day presentation.

(Two girls are on their way to church on Easter Sunday morning to participate in the Easter program. They meet people along the way and practice their speeches on them.)

(Mother calls to Alicia from offstage. Alicia is sitting on a bench stage right.)

Mother: Alicia, Alicia, where are you?

Alicia: Mother, I'm outside. It's such a beautiful day.

Mother: So it is. You ready to give your speech?

Alicia: Yes. Can we go now? I'm supposed to be there at least an hour before the play.

Mother: Let's go. You really look pretty, Alicia. And I'm so proud of you. *(Telephone rings.)* I forgot my cell phone in the house. Let me go get it. Then I'll drive you to church. *(Kim is walking by on her way to church.)*

Alicia: Hi, Kim. You want to ride with us to church?

Kim: No, thanks. I'll walk.

Alicia: Wait. Let me see if I can walk with you. *(She exits right. Kim walks toward the bench and just as she's about to sit down, Brother Joseph, who lives next door to Alicia, enters from left. He has a newspaper in his hands.)*

Bro. Joseph: Why, if it isn't Miss Kim. Don't you look lovely in your pretty dress.

Kim: Thanks, Brother Joseph.

Bro. Joseph: Guess you're on your way to church.

Kim: Yes, got to give my Easter speech. My mama helped me learn it. You want to hear it?

Bro. Joseph: Sure, I do. *(He sits while Kim recites her speech.)*

Kim: Jesus was hung in the middle with a thief on each side—two thieves and a Savior who from sin none could hide. However, one thief recognized his wrong-headed ways.

And Jesus promised him brighter days. Jesus did no wrong, but he died for you and me. We all need salvation, and God gives us mercy. So on the third day, when he rose from the grave, he opened heaven so we could know God's amazing grace.

Bro. Joseph: *(Brother Joseph claps.)* Very good, young lady. Now that's a good message that everybody needs to hear.

Kim: The second verse is really somebody else's part, but Miss Owens told me to learn it just in case.

Bro. Joseph: That's because you're extra smart! *(Alicia reenters.)* Alicia, you got a speech?

Alicia: Yes, sir.

Bro. Joseph: Let me hear it.

Alicia: Brother Joseph, my mother said you have to come back to church if you want to hear my speech.

Bro. Joseph: I was at sunrise service this morning at 6:00 a.m. And we sho' had a good time in the Lord. The preacher delivered a good message about how God allowed his only Son, Jesus, to be born so he could die for our sins. And I'm glad he did, too. Because I was sho' 'nuff a sinner. I was a drunk. But I feel like I been resurrected! And now I just thank God that Jesus is a friend of mine.

Kim: Please come, Brother Joseph! Please!

Bro. Joseph: Can't make no promises. Ya'll run along and make me proud.

Alicia: Come on, Kim. I can walk with you. My mother has to run an errand before comin' to church. *(They start walking. They sing "He Arose" as they go.)*

Kim: I'm so thirsty.

Alicia: We can get some water when we get to the church.

Kim: No, I want to stop by Miss Julia's and get me a cold soda.

Alicia: I'm not supposed to go into that house.

Kim: It will only take a minute and nobody has to know.

Alicia: Kim, we're supposed to go straight to church.

Kim: I'll be right back. *(She exits left. Alicia hollers at her.)*

Alicia: See you at the church. I'm not getting into trouble on Easter Day. *(She starts walking toward the church and runs into one of her schoolmates, Victoria, who is jumping rope.)* Hey, Victoria. How you doing?

Victoria: I'm doing just fine. I like your Easter dress.

Alicia: Thanks. You'd better run and get dressed. I want you to hear my speech.

Victoria: No, my mother, she got laid off. She didn't have any money to get me a dress.

Alicia: Well, wear one of your old dresses. My mother said that Easter is not about getting new clothes. It's about Jesus, and how he died for our sins.

Victoria: And how he rose again early on Easter morning. Well, I got to run.

Alicia: Victoria, can I do my speech for you?

Victoria: OK, I guess I can wait.

Alicia: Jesus died before their eyes, their tears flowed down and covered the ground. They buried him in a borrowed tomb, as heads hung low and were full of gloom. They'd loved him so much. He'd loved them, too. But they didn't know just what to do. They retired to their homes and made further preparation to anoint his dead body for a long separation. Early Sunday morning, the women rushed to the tomb. With fear in their eyes, they didn't believe what they saw. Sitting atop the rolled away stone was an angel who said,"Jesus is gone! Fear not, you see, for Jesus is risen!"

Victoria: That was good. I wish I could be in the play.

Alicia: Victoria, I'll trade my new dress for one of your old ones if you'll come to our program today. Maybe even. . .*(She begins to whisper in Victoria's ear. They exit left as an off-stage voice hollers at Kim.)*

OSF voice: Get on away from here. I don't want to hear that Jesus mess. *(Kim reenters from left, followed by Miss Julia.)*

Miss Julia: Child, like I said before, don't pay her no mind. I want to hear your speech. So you just go right on ahead. I'll hold your soda. *(Kim recites her speech.)*

Kim: Jesus was hung in the middle with a thief on each side—two thieves and a Savior, who from sin none could hide. However, one thief recognized his wrong-headed ways. And Jesus promised him brighter days. Jesus did no wrong, but he died for you and me. We all need salvation, and God gives us mercy. So on the third day, when he rose from the grave, he opened heaven so we could know God's amazing grace.

Miss Julia: That was good, Kim. *(She gives her back her drink and money.)* Here, take your money back. I used to go to church, but after my mother died I was mad at the world. I did not believe that God could love me and take my mother. *(She starts to cry. Kim hugs her.)*

Kim: Don't cry. God does love you. Jesus came so that we could have life! Why don't you come to our program today?

Miss Julia: I don't know. It's been so long.

Kim: Please come.

Miss Julia: You know, I think I just might.

Kim: *(Looks at watch.)* Oh my goodness, I've got to get to the church. So I'll see you there. *(Miss Julia exits left as Kim walks right, toward the church. Alicia and Victoria reenter. Victoria has on Alicia's beautiful dress.)*

Alicia: Hey, Kim.

Kim: Alicia, girl, I thought you'd be at the church by now. Why is she wearing your dress? You are gonna be in trouble!

Alicia: Ah, it will be all right. Victoria is coming to church with us.

Kim: Hi, Victoria. I just hope your mother doesn't kill you.

Alicia: She won't. She's always talking about how Jesus gave his life for us on the cross. So today is a day of giving just like Christmas Day. (*They exit right.)*

(Easter music plays as the stage area is being decorated for the Easter play. Remove bicycle, etc. from the stage. The stage is now divided into two halves. At left, the modern-day recitations take place near the cross. At right, the biblical day scenes take place. At downstage right are four chairs and a table to be used by the women of Jesus' day. Upstage right, the

women are crying in front of Jesus' tomb. The characters who are witnessing the Easter presentation will sit in the first few pews with the rest of the audience. They will move toward the stage when it is their time to speak. The play director, Miss Owens, enters from left.)

Miss Owens: Good afternoon and happy Easter Day. We are so happy that you've come out to help us celebrate our resurrected Lord. We are going back in time to the hours after Jesus' Crucifixion, and the Resurrection morning. Church, the good news is that "He got up!"

Narrator: Over two thousand years ago, a man named Jesus walked this earth. He was a gentle being who ministered to the masses. He healed the sick, raised the dead, and challenged the religious leaders of his day. He tried to open their eyes to a new way of seeing and a new way of being. Some people really experienced resurrected lives even before Jesus died. Our play begins just after Jesus Christ's death.
(Joseph of Arimathea and Nicodemus enter from right. The three Marys and Salome are at left crying in front of a cave upstage right. A soldier stands guard.)

Joseph: Ladies, as you can see, the tomb is sealed. Nicodemus and I did the best we could. We anointed his body with myrrh and aloes and wrapped the linen shroud around him. I still can't believe that he is gone. It just doesn't seem real.

Mary Mag.: Joseph, we'd like to thank you and Nicodemus. We don't know what we would have done without you.

Mary, Joses: Thanks for being bold enough to step forward and beg Pilate for his body.

Mary Mag.: And for putting him in your new tomb. That was so unselfish of you.

Joseph: I had to. He'd done so much for me. After I met Jesus, I knew God was truly with me. He taught me how to live. His teachings breathed new life into me. *(Mary, mother of Jesus, cries out, "Jesus!")* And I will be there for you too, Mary. I don't want you to worry about anything.

Soldier: All right, let's move along now! *(Gruffly.)*

Salome: We'd better be getting Mary home. She needs to eat and rest. Come along, Mary. *(They all exit right.)*

Song: "Were You There When They Crucified My Lord?"

(The three Marys enter from right. They are making preparation for the sabbath and for anointing Jesus' body on Sunday morning. Mary, mother of Jesus, is sitting alone at left.)

Mary Mag.: Salome should be back with food in a few minutes. It is almost time for our blessed sabbath rest.

Mary, Jesus: It's so hard to believe that he is dead. It was too cruel for words. Even with all of his suffering, he still took time to make sure I'd be all right. I can still hear him telling me to look at John as my son. And for John to look at me as his mother. *(Salome enters with some bread.)*

Salome: I was able to get some bread from a friend up the street. Here, Mary, at least eat a piece of bread. Everyone is talking about the Crucifixion. Our lives will never be the same. *(Scene cuts back over to modern day.)*

Kim: Jesus was hung in the middle with a thief on each side—two thieves and a Savior who from sin none could hide. However, one thief recognized his wrong-headed ways. And Jesus promised him brighter days.

Young Boy: Jesus did no wrong, but he died for you and me. We all need salvation, and God gives us mercy. So on the third day, when he rose from the grave, he opened heaven so we could know God's amazing grace. *(Back to biblical times.)*

Mary, Jesus: My mind just keeps running back to happier moments with Jesus. He was such a wonderful baby, and he grew into such a wonderful man. But there was so much about him I didn't understand. There were so many things that amazed me. I just kept much of it here in my heart. Remember the time we went to Jerusalem for the Feast of the Passover?

Mary, Joses: He was twelve, wasn't he?

Mary, Jesus: We were on our way home. A day had passed and we thought he was with other family members, but he was nowhere to be found. We found him in the Temple a couple of days later.

Mary, Joses: Sitting there listening and asking questions of the teachers.

Mary, Jesus: I remember him saying, "Why were you worried? Didn't you know that I must be about my Father's business." So many memories…

Mary Mag.: And there were so many good ones, too. Before today…

Mary, Joses: We did a lot of traveling, didn't we? And there was Martha and her sister, Mary, always trying to prepare for the arrival of Jesus and his friends. You know what I liked most about Jesus? He was always so kind and compassionate. He even cried when he heard that their brother had died. Remember how he raised Lazarus from the dead? *(Cut over to modern day.)*

All: Another resurrected life! *(Back to biblical times.)*

Mary Mag.: Jesus. He changed my life in so many ways. I was physically ill, and my money did me no good. I was possessed by at least seven demons. Who knows what I did being so troubled. But Jesus didn't care about all that I had done wrong. He saw the real Mary. He made me feel like I was valuable, and he never once looked down on me. He took the time to heal everything that was wrong with me, and now I'm a new Mary. He made me believe in myself again. And there was nothing I loved more that being a servant in his movement.

Mary, Joses: And that is what Jesus was all about, wasn't it? Serving God and people. *(She walks over to Mary.)* Come, Mary, you need to get some rest. *(They exit left.)*

Mary Mag.: He also once said that he came not to be served, but to serve. I'm gonna miss him so much. *(Pause.)* For him to end up this way. *(She cries.)*

Salome: I know. We'll get some more spices tomorrow evening just as soon as the sabbath ends. And we'll go to the tomb as early as possible. We'd better get some rest. *(They exit left.) (Scene cuts back over to modern day.)*

Alicia: Jesus died before their eyes. Their tears flowed down and covered the ground. They buried him in a borrowed tomb, as heads hung low and were full of gloom. They'd loved him so much. He'd loved them, too. But they didn't know just what to do. They retired to their homes and made further preparation to anoint his dead body for a long separation. *(Back to biblical times. It's early Sunday morning. Mary Magdalene; Mary, mother of Joses; and Salome hurry to Jesus' tomb.)*

Mary Mag.: Hurry, hurry. But who is going to roll the stone away? That soldier was not very nice!

Mary, Joses: Ladies, look. The stone has been rolled away. *(They act as if they're peering into the tomb.)*

All Marys: I see. I see.

Angel: "Do not be alarmed. You seek Jesus of Nazareth, who was crucified. He is risen! He is not here. See the place where they laid him. But, go tell his disciples—and Peter—that he is going before you into Galilee; there you will see him, as he said to you." *(Scene returns to modern day.)*

Victoria: Early Sunday morning, the women rushed to the tomb with fear in their eyes. They didn't believe what they saw—sitting atop the rolled-away stone was an angel who said, "Jesus is gone! Fear not, you see, for Jesus is risen!"

Kindergarten class: He got up, up from the grave. *(Lines can be divided.)* A resurrected life we all can have. Roll the stones of sin away and have new life this Easter Day! *(Back to biblical times.)*

Mary Mag.: He said he'd rise again. Oh dear, we've got to run and tell the others. *(They exit left, running and praising God.)*

Narrator: And Jesus rose that first Easter morn centuries ago, to give us a chance at a new life. For he'd paid the price on Calvary's hill. All left now is to do God's will. He lives, Church. He lives in each of us. He is our Savior! *(Applause while Miss Owens enters from left.)*

Miss Owens: Let's give our participants another round of applause. I'm so proud of each of them, and thank you all for coming. *(Alicia, Kim, and Victoria stand at left looking out at the audience. Miss Julia stands and moves forward.)*

Kim: Miss Julia came, Alicia. Let's go over and say hello. *(Alicia's father walks over to them.)*

Alicia: Daddy, you got off from work!

Stan Carter: I told you I'd be here. Nice job, young ladies. *(He hugs them all.)* Excuse me. See you all in the fellowship hall. *(He exits right. Miss Julia walks over to them.)*

Miss Julia: Kim, Alicia, and Victoria, you all did such a nice job. Thanks, Kim, for inviting me here today. I've decided to give my life back to Christ. *(Alicia's mother hugs her.)*

Mother: Julia, I'm so glad to hear you say that. Another resurrected life! Alicia, your speech was great. I'm so proud of all of you. When did you learn those lines, Victoria? And that dress looks great on you. Why don't you keep it?

Victoria: For real? Thanks, Mrs. Carter. *(Bro. Joseph comes over.)*

Alicia: Bro. Joseph, I'm so glad you came.

Bro. Joseph: I'm so glad I came. Ya'll reminded me about how good Jesus has been to me. I can relate to Mary Magdalene because I was sho' 'nuff a sinner. I was a drunk, I tell you. But I gave my life to Jesus, and I'm living in the power of his resurrection!

Alicia: This has been such a wonderful Easter program. Let's get some refreshments. *(They walk right, toward the exit.)*

The End

THE UNDERGROUND RESURRECTION

by Valeria Steele Roberson

CAST:

Harriet Tubman: A former slave who went South numerous times to deliver others from slavery.

Louisa: A young slave girl who is very curious

Clara: Louisa's very emotional mother

Charles: A young slave who was whipped many times by his master

MacRay: An older slave who is very wise

Ruth: A character from the Bible *(can be played by a teen)*

Isaiah: An ex-slave named after the character from the Bible

Daniel: A character from the Bible

Non-Speaking Parts: Mary Magdalene; Salome; Mary, Mother of James; Angel

PROP LIST

Harriet's knapsack that includes a loaf of bread, a water container, a jar of salve, and a gun.
Bale of hay
Shoes for Charles
Blankets
Old rags for bandages
Basket full of food and water containers

SET: (The play opens as Harriet and her passengers are trying to hide from slave catchers. They're hiding in a barn with a concealed floor at the William Randolph farm in Buffalo, New York. Place a bale of hay at right.)

TIME: At sunrise, it is Friday, two days before Easter and everybody is asleep. Harriet wakes up and moves stage right away from the group and begins praying into a hole in the ground.

SCENE I

Harriet: Oh, Lord, I need you to help us. Lord, we thank you for allowing us to reach this safe place in Buffalo, New Yawk. You done brought us all the way from Maryland. And, Lord, now we's so close. Just a few more miles 'til we gets to Canada, to freedom. Please guide us to safety, Lord. Let your North Star shine! We thank you for deliverance right now. In the sweet name of Jesus, your Son and our miracle worker, I pray. Amen. *(MacRay walks over to her.)*

MacRay: Can't sleep, Miss Harriet?

Harriet: Too excited. First of all, I'm happy that ya'll gonna be free. An' second, this marks two days before Easter Sunday morning. I don't like thinking too much 'bout Jesus sufferin' on the cross. But what comes after makes me want to shout.

MacRay: Jesus done rose from the grave. Miss Harriet, knowing Jesus was the onliest thing kept me going all of these years. *(Louisa wakes up and then wakes up her mother.)*

Louisa: Mama, I had a bad dream. They caught us and... *(She begins to cry.)*

Clara: Don't cry, baby girl. We's safe here in Mr. Randolph's barn. Don't nobody know 'bout this room hidden 'neath his barn. And don't you know that Miss Harriet ain't never got caught. An' she never will. *(Charles thrashes and talks in his sleep.)*

Charles: Yes sir, master, I ain't gonna do it no mo.' *(Clara shakes him out of his sleep.)*

Clara: Wake up, Charles, it's all right. You won't have to be scared no mo' when we get to Canada.

Charles: I sho' hope so. *(Harriet and MacRay walk over to them. Harriet offers them all a piece of bread to munch on and some water.)*

Louisa: Thanks, Miss Harriet. *(Others say thanks, too.)*

Harriet: Ya'll go on back to sleep. Tonight we be travelin' in the back of a wagon most of the night.

Louisa: Miss Harriet, will you tell us a story?

(As Harriet enacts the story at left, actors can be acting it out at right.)

Harriet: A story. Well, since it's Easter time, I'll tell you 'bout the women who ran to the tomb early that blessed Sunday mornin'. There was Mary Magdalene, Salome, and the other Mary who went there to anoint the body of Jesus. But what they found instead was God's miracle. You see, there was a great earthquake, and an angel rolled the stone away an' told 'em not to be afraid. Say, "Jesus is not here, for he done rose up!" After they saw that he wasn't there, the angel told 'em to tell the rest of 'em, you know, the men folk, the good news. And they ran to tell 'em.

MacRay: Sho' 'nuff. Only a powerful God like ourns could have done sumpin' like that.

Harriet: But that's not all. The Bible says that some of God's saints who had been asleep got up after Jesus rose and walked around the city an' appeared to people.

Charles: Are you saying that dead folk got up and walked around? *(Harriet nods yes.)* That must have been a sight.

Harriet: Now, Charles, they wasn't trying to scare nobody. They were just witnessin' to God's power. *(Charles yawns.)*

Charles: I better get me some more shut-eye.

Louisa: I'm sleepy too. *(Louisa and Charles go back to their pallets.)*

Harriet: I guess that Charles don't believe that God can work a miracle.

MacRay: Well, I know He can.

Clara: I believe God can do anything. This is God's world.

Harriet: I had one of my sleeping fits a few weeks back; and whilst I was in it, I had a dream. I was in a dark place. All'a sudden a light shone brightly in the distance. I walked toward that light, and there she stood.

Clara: Who?

Harriet: Ruth! She's one of my favorite Bible people because our stories are sort of alike. It takes a lot of faith to leave the known for the unknown. Anyway, this is what I heard and saw. *(Ruth enters from left. Harriet rises and joins her. She sits down before Ruth.)*

Ruth: Keep looking up to God, Harriet. He'll be there for you just like He was there for my dear, sweet mother-in-law, Naomi, and me.

Harriet: He helped you do the right thing for your life, didn't He?

Ruth: He sure did. I loved my mother-in-law, Naomi, so much. When she told me she was returning to Bethlehem, I knew I had to go with her. By that time, I realized who God was. I knew I could depend on God. So I took a step in faith, and God blessed me beyond my imagination. You just never know what will happen when you serve the true and living God.

Harriet: Is it true that you were resurrected with Jesus?

Ruth: Oh, yes, Harriet. I was there on that happy day. We walked around Jerusalem telling everybody we saw about God's awesome power. Be encouraged, dear sister. Keep trusting in God. *(She exits right and then Harriet rejoins the others and sits down.)*

Harriet: Then I woke up.

Clara: Our God is still in the miracle-making business. Please, Lord, help us just like you helped Ruth.

MacRay: Praise be to God.

Harriet: We'd better get some sleep. We got a long night ahead. *(Blackout or play music to indicate the change of scenes.)*

SCENE II

(It's Saturday, the next evening. It's the night before Easter. Harriet and the others are moving up Freedom's Highway through the bushes.)

Clara: I don't means to complain or nothin', but it sho' was nice to travel in that wagon last night.

Louisa: I'm so tired, Mama.

Harriet: I know ya'll is tired. We don't have that much farther to go. Our next stop is on top of that hill.

Clara: Thank goodness. Don't know if'n I can walk much farther. My feets hurtin' already!

Charles: Me neither. I can see it. *(Points right.)* Come on, ya'll, I'm hungry.

Harriet: Get back in line.

Charles: Why? We can see it ain't far. *(Harriet pulls out her gun.)*

Harriet: I'm not lettin' you mess this up. Get back. *(Shh.)*

MacRay: What is it, Harriet?

Harriet: Just a feeling. Let's hide over there. *(They move left and pretend like they're hiding. Then they hear horses on the road. Harriet moves right and looks where the horses are going.)* Oh, my Lord, that was too close for comfort. We'll wait here 'til it's good an' dark. Then I'll go and scout out the place. Have a seat ev'rybody and get comf'table.

Charles: I'm real sorry, Miss Harriet.

MacRay: He told you, didn't he?

Harriet: Yes, it was Jesus. I always get this feeling when danger is near.

Louisa: What does it feel like?

Harriet: I can't really explain it.

Clara: God will do that for His chil'ren.

MacRay: Praise be to God. Takin' care of us, even when we act like we ain't got no sense.

Charles: I done said I was sorry. *(He steps on a spiny sweet gum burr.)* Oh, I…my foot.

Harriet: Shh. Shh. A burr got you. Let me take a look at your foot. It's pretty bad. I betta put some of my salve on that. *(She removes jar from bag and places some salve on his foot.)* You rest now. *(Charles lies down.)*

Charles: Those things sho' put a hurtin' on your foots. I gots to get me some shoes. Can't go no farther 'til I do.

Harriet: I'll see 'bout it in the mornin'. Too many slave catchers round now.

MacRay: It's always somethin' in dis here life. That's why the Good Lawd says to take it one day at a time. Charles, we gwine get you just what you needs. God will see to it.

Harriet: Let's get comf'table.

Louisa: Miss Harriet, can you tell us a story?

Harriet: If you all don't mind hearing about some more Bible peoples, I can.

MacRay: Help yo'self.

Harriet: It seems like whenever I need some encouragement, God sends me some body. One time He sent me one of the greatest prophets ever—Isaiah.

Louisa: Was he one of those saints who rose when Jesus rose from the dead?

Harriet: Sho' was. He believed mens should depend on God and not live by fear.

MacRay: Only a powerful God can raise people from the dead.

Clara: So what do you think Isaiah said to the people after he rose up?

Harriet: For one thing, Clara, I think he talked about how Jesus can heal these old bodies.

Charles: I wish.

MacRay: Don't it say in Isaiah: "By his stripes we are healed?" They sho' put a lot of them on him, too, before they nailed him to de cross. Jesus was beat just like we was. *(A man begins singing the spiritual, "Swing Low," off-stage right.)*

Harriet: Shh. Shh. Be very quiet. *(The man continues to sing. Harriet walks toward the singing. She exits right.)*

Clara: Lord, have mercy, where she done gone?

MacRay: It will be all right, Li'l Sister. *(Harriet enters followed by Isaiah.)*

Harriet: Ya'll, this here is Isaiah. Mr. Jones from up the road sent him down here to look for us. Ain't he a sight for sore eyes?

Isaiah: I got a wagon just a ways off through that brush over there. Follow me, and I take you to Mr. Jones' barn up on the hill.

Clara: God sho' answers prayers.

MacRay: Always on time. Here, lean on me, Charles.

Charles: Thank goodness. *(They follow Isaiah and exit right.)*

SCENE III

(Harriet and the others follow Isaiah into Mr. Jones' barn. There are a few blankets scattered about. They are sitting around talking.)

(Isaiah begins to laugh.)

Isaiah: Ya'll be safe here in Mr. Jones' barn. Right here is a basket full of food and water.

Harriet: Thank you so much, Isaiah. Ya'll, Isaiah been free 'bout ten years now.

Louisa: We almost free too, ain't we, Mama?

Clara: Yeah, that's right.

Isaiah: Ain't nothing like it. I still can't believe that you were just about to tell them about the prophet Isaiah when I showed up.

Louisa: How you get your name, Isaiah?

Isaiah: My mama named me after the prophet, Isaiah. She loved all he had to say about Jesus. How Jesus loved the poor and cared about the brokenhearted. How he'd give sight to the blind and deliverance to captives. How he came to make a difference in people's lives. People like you and like me. You see, we knows how all of that feels. We knows about going without. But Jesus, he came to make life better for us all.

Clara: You sho' seem to know the Bible. Can you read?

Isaiah: Yes, mam, I sho' can.

Louisa: Mama, can I learn to read?

Isaiah: Child, you sho' will. Just keep your hands in God's hands. All things are possible for God.

MacRay: Sho' 'nuff. 'Cause Jesus died on that cross.

Isaiah: He was despised and rejected by men, a bearer of our griefs and a carrier of our sorrows. He took it all on that cross with him. Yes, Jesus was our sin-bearing servant. Now, that comes from the prophet Isaiah.

MacRay: And then Jesus rose again on the third day.

Isaiah: Yes, so it is by stripes we are healed.

Harriet: See, Charles, Jesus will heal your feet. He can heal all of our illnesses. One time I was so sick, didn't nobody think I'd make it. So when all around you seems so dark in your life, have faith 'cause God can do ev'rything but fail.

MacRay: Amen.

Isaiah: *(He rises.)* Well, I better be goin'. Ya'll are safe here. Just a few more miles, and ya'll be in Canada. Ya'll can leave here tomorrow night. Miss Harriet, ya'll be careful now. God go with you.

Louisa: Thank you, Mr. Isaiah.

Isaiah: Ya'll is welcome. God bless all of you. *(He exits right.)*

Harriet: Let's get some rest. *(They all go to sleep.)*

SCENE IV

(It's the next morning, Sunday, around dawn. All are still sleeping. Harriet enters from right with a pair of shoes and some food to eat.)

Harriet: It's another Easter mornin' sunrise and I'm glad 'bout it. Lawd, we just want to give you thanks for Jesus Christ who suffered, died, and rose from the grave. And Lawd, we thank you that this is Resurrection Day for all these chil'ren you give me to take across to the free side. In Jesus the Christ's name we pray. Amen. *(The others start rising as Harriet moves closer to them.)*

MacRay: Miss Harriet, happy Easter Day.

Harriet: Same to you.

Louisa: Miss Harriet, tonight is the night, right?

Harriet: We almost there. I got ya'll some food, and here's some water, too. So eat up. Charles, here you some shoes.

Charles: Thank you, Miss Harriet.

Harriet: How your feet doin' today?

Charles: Why, Miss Harriet, they's just like new.

Harriet: I told you that Jesus is a healer.

MacRay: Amen. Always give us just what we need.

Clara: Are you sure we should try tonight?

Harriet: Child, we'll see. God didn't bring us this far to leave us.

MacRay: No, siree. No more slave days and slave ways. We be delivered just like Daniel from the lions' den.

Louisa: Tell 'em Miss Harriet, tell 'em.

Harriet: Louisa wants me to tell you about my dream about the prophet Daniel.

Louisa: And he rose on that day when Jesus rose, didn't he, Miss Harriet?

Harriet: Why 'course he did. Daniel tried to encourage his people during a time when they were slaves, just like so many of our people are. One of his messages was that God...

MacRay: was still in control no matter what their lot in life.

Harriet: That's right.

Clara: That's good to hear.

Harriet: Better to know. We have to live by faith, not sight.

Charles: Tell us more about Daniel.

Harriet: When Daniel came upon some people after he'd risen from the dead, he had a very important message for them. *(Daniel enters from left.)*

Daniel: God is a good God. God delivered me again and again. Just look at me. I'm a living, breathing testimony of His goodness once more in the land of the living. So don't be scared of me. I just got a few more things I'd like to tell you. Many years ago, I lived in exile in Babylon, and it was a very trying time for me and my friends. However, there is one time in particular that I'll never forget. One time I slept in the lions' den all night long. I ended up there because I prayed to my God three times a day. I didn't care about a new law that said I couldn't pray. And God shut the lions' jaws, and they left me alone. So I know that when you are faithful to God, He'll see you through. *(Daniel exits left.)*

MacRay: Amen.

Harriet: Isn't God good? It's just a few more hours' journey before ya'll be in Canada. We'll leave when night falls. All I ask is that you all keep God first and always help somebody else in this life.

Louisa: We will, won't we, Mama? Miss Harriet, thank you so much for ev'rything. *(They all thank Ms. Harriet.)*

Harriet: It's like the Good Book says, "A child shall lead them." God bless you, child. God bless you all. This Easter, ya'll gon' be delivered! *(Starts singing "They Rolled the Stone Away" or another song about Easter.)*

The End

THEY ROLLED THE STONE AWAY: An Easter Rap

by Michael Walker

CAST:

Leader

Group member (Group Mem.)

Group

> **INSTRUCTIONS:** Each group should make up its own steps and rhythmic beats to this rap drill.

Leader: *(Speaking to group. This line is a call to order for the group.)* Do you have stones that seem to block your path?

Group Mem.: Yes, there are stones in my way!

Leader: Did you know that he died and rose in three days despite a great stone blocking his path?

Group Mem.: Yes, we do, but who rolled the stone away?

Leader: Matthew 28:2 says, "And suddenly there was a great earthquake; for an angel of the Lord, descending from heaven, came and rolled back the stone and sat on it."

Group Mem.: Luke 24:2 says, "They found the stone rolled away from the tomb." So who rolled the stone away?

Leader: They rolled the stone away!

Group: Who were they? Were they angels?

Leader: They rolled the stone away!

Group: Who were they? Were they friends of Jesus?

Leader: They rolled that old stone away!

Group: Who were they? How did they roll that stone away?

Leader: They rolled that stone away by the power of God! Who are we?

Group: Believers!

Leader: How do we roll the stones away?

Group: Faith!

Leader: How?

Group: Trust!

Leader: How?

Group: By the power of God!

Leader: With faith and trust, we will move the stones of sin, hatred, guilt, and malice. We will replace them with love and joy! *(The group acts out the moving of stones and shows joy and love for one another.)* Who are we?

Group: Believers with faith and trust!

Leader: Mary didn't weep and Martha ceased to moan. Why?

Group: They believed with faith and trust.

Leader: They rolled the stone away! Who?

Group: Angels and believers with faith and trust!

Leader: Who will roll the old stones away?

Group: We, the believers, with our faith and trust.

Leader: What stones can we move?

Group: Any stone that stands in our way!

Leader: How?

Group: With faith, trust, love, and joy! By the power of God!

Leader: Who will roll the stones away?

All: We, the true believers, with faith and trust! By the power of God!

The End

PRESCHOOL/KINDERGARTEN

by Karen Williams

Listen, everybody.

Listen, everybody.

To what I have to say,

Jesus isn't in the grave;

He's alive this Easter Day!

BIG NEWS

by Karen Williams

Child One: I know I'm small, but my news is big. *(Stretches arms wide to indicate big.)* Jesus died for us all!

Child Two: And I may not be nine or ten, but one thing I know, Jesus rose again. *(Lifts arms in a raising fashion.)*

Ages 6-8

EASTER

by Karen Williams

(This is a group recitation with six children. Each child holds one letter of the word EASTER.)

E: E is for Eternal life Jesus offers to those who will believe.

A: A is for All the miracles Jesus performed for those who would receive.

S: S is for the Soldiers who blocked his grave with a heavy stone.

T: T is for the Tomb where they placed Jesus. They thought he was dead and gone.

E: E is for Everyone—for all of us the cross Jesus bore.

R: R is for Resurrection—Jesus is alive for evermore!

BRAND NEW!

by Karen Williams

(Chorus can consist of several children.)

Child One: Now, don't we all look our best?

Chorus: Brand new! Brand new!

Child One: New clothes, new shoes, and all the rest!

Chorus: Brand new! Brand new!

Child Two: But the new life Jesus gives can't be bought in the mall.

Chorus: Brand new! Brand new!

Child Two: He died and rose to save us all!

Chorus: Brand new! Brand new!

Child Three: If we are in Christ the old is gone, and the new has come.

All Children: Brand new! Brand new!

AGES 9-12

SIMON OF CYRENE

by Karen Williams

Speaker One: There was a man name Simon, who was from a city called Cyrene. One day while in Jerusalem, he saw an awful scene. A huge crowd lined the street, people of all degrees. There were Romans, Jews, priests, and Pharisees. Simon saw people crying, saying, "Jesus has done no wrong." He heard others mock Jesus as they traveled in a throng.

Speaker Two: Then Simon saw Jesus, the Savior, who had fallen on the ground. Jesus wore twisted thorns on which his head was crowned. And right beside him on the ground, a cross lay in full view. You see the cross is for criminals, and all the wrong they do.

Speaker Three: But Jesus was no criminal, he only did what was good. He showed love and healed the sick throughout the neigborhood. Simon could not bear to see the Savior suffer so. He began to walk away for he felt that he must go.

Speaker Four: Then a Roman soldier pointed at Simon, and his words were at a loss. When the soldier said, "Hey you, get over here and carry that cross." Simon was shocked and afraid; he hesitated and doubted. "You heard what I said, get that cross now," the soldier shouted. So Simon picked up the cross, which was as heavy as steel. And he carried it for Jesus all the way up Golgotha Hill.

Speaker One: "Father, forgive them," Jesus said, "for they know not what they do." So they crucified the Savior, who was placed between thief one and two.

Speaker Two: But the cross was no defeat, no, that's not the end of the story. For Jesus rose on the third day in all his glory.

Speaker Three: What Simon experienced that day, he never shall forget—he carried the cross for Jesus, and he had no regrets.

Speaker Four: We, like Simon, have a cross to bear, every one of us, don't you see?

Speaker One: For to be a disciple, Jesus said, "Take up the cross and follow me."